Making Animal BABIES

Sneed B. Collard III • Illustrated by Steve Jenkins

HOUGHTON MIFFLIN COMPANY

BOSTON 2000

For Steve and Carol,
and the great babies they've made.
Much love,
Sneed

For Jamie —S.J.

Text copyright © 2000 by Sneed B. Collard III
Illustrations copyright © 2000 by Steve Jenkins

The text of this book is set in Adobe Garamond.
The illustrations are cut-paper collage.

Library of Congress Cataloging-in-Publication Data

Collard, Sneed B.
Making animal babies / by Sneed B. Collard III ; illustrated by Steve Jenkins.
p.   cm.
Summary: Describes the mating rituals and reproductive methods of a variety of animals,
including flatworms, jellyfish, chameleons, and walruses.
ISBN 0-395-95317-0
1. Reproduction—Juvenile literature. [1. Reproduction. 2. Animals—Courtship.]
I. Jenkins, Steve, 1952–   ill.
II. Title
QP251.5.C65   2000
571.8'1—dc21
99-35797
CIP

Manufactured in the United States of America
WOZ 10 9 8 7 6 5 4 3 2 1

Animals make babies in many ways.

They bud.

Buds don't grow only on plants. They also grow on some ocean animals. Sea squirts, sponges, and sea anemones all make babies—or reproduce—by *budding*. Buds are special clumps of cells that grow out of the bodies of their parents. Once a bud grows to a certain size or age, the parent sheds or releases it. It's now a new animal able to live and grow all on its own.

They split.

When certain kinds of brittle stars grow large enough, they divide down the middle and split into smaller "twins." Each twin grows new arms to become another complete brittle star. Certain types of flatworms, sea stars, sea cucumbers, and anemones also reproduce by splitting. Scientists call this kind of reproduction *fission*.

They "break."

As they move about, some kinds of sea anemones *fragment.* Little pieces separate from an anemone's base and grow into new animals. Fragmentation is different from budding. Buds are special groups of cells designed to grow into new animals. Fragments are just pieces of the parent that "break off."

And they stack up, too.

These jellyfish babies grow stacked on top of one another. Younger jellies form on the bottom of the stack and are pushed up, assembly-line style. Over time, the oldest jellies pop off the top and grow into adult jellyfish.

Budding, fission, fragmentation, and stacking are all forms of *asexual reproduction*. In asexual reproduction, one parent makes babies that are exactly the same as itself. These identical babies are called *clones*.

But most animals make babies by *sexual reproduction.*

In *sexual reproduction*, the traits of two parent animals are mixed together. Their babies—unlike clones—end up with a combination of traits that is different from that of either parent.

Sexual reproduction happens when two different cells, a *sperm* and an *egg*, join together. Usually, the sperm comes from a male parent or "dad," and the egg comes from a female parent or "mom."

Sperm are extremely small—more than 400 million human sperm can fit into a teaspoon. *Eggs* are much larger—but in most cases they are still too small to see without a microscope. Sperm are made in reproductive organs called *testes*. Eggs are made in *ovaries*. Some worms and other animals have both testes and ovaries in the same individual. But for most animals—including people—testes are found only in males and ovaries are found only in females. That's why it usually takes both a mom and a dad to make a baby.

Once a sperm enters an egg, together they form a new living thing, which will grow and grow into a baby. But in a big world, how do a tiny sperm and egg ever get together?

When a sperm penetrates, or enters, an egg, it is called *fertilization*. Fertilization is important because a sperm and an egg each contain only half of the material it takes to make a baby. Without fertilization by the sperm, eggs from most kinds of animals could never grow into babies.

Many sea animals launch their sperm and eggs right into the water, where some of them find each other.

At certain times of year, surgeonfish and other kinds of tropical fish *spawn*. Males and females release their sperm and eggs—billions of them—into the water. Many drift away by themselves or get eaten by other hungry animals. But some sperm come into contact with some eggs and fertilize them. The young embryos grow and develop as they drift about in their soft egg enclosures. Many kinds of corals, worms, clams, and other sea animals also reproduce by spawning.

But most animals have to find a partner to mate with, and that's not always easy.

Some animals show flashy colors to attract a partner.

Chameleons are lizards that have special cells called *chromatophores* in their skin. These chromatophores allow the lizards to change their colors and patterns. Chameleons usually blend in with their surroundings, but during mating season a male "brightens up" to attract females.

Others fight to win a partner.

When walruses gather together each winter, males use their three-foot-long tusks to fight for the right to mate. The battles can be fierce, but each winner gains control of a harem of females to mate with. By winning females and mating with them, a male makes sure that his own family line will survive.

Others build to impress a partner.

Male bower birds build elaborate arches, domes, and other structures out of twigs, grasses, and leaves. These creations are called bowers. The bower's only purpose is to impress females, and each male decorates his bower with brightly colored flowers and other showy objects. Like a picky shopper, the female inspects a number of bowers and chooses the male with the best bower to be her mate.

And some simply light up the sky.

Fireflies communicate using light. To find a mate, the male patrols the evening sky, flashing his tail lamp every few seconds. A female answers by flashing her own signal until the male lands next to her to mate. Every kind, or *species*, of firefly has its own system of flashing signals. This prevents a firefly from mating with fireflies of other species.

Once a male and female choose each other, they mate. Different animals mate in different ways. In some animals, the female releases her eggs as the male releases his sperm over them.

To mate, a male frog grasps a female "piggyback." As the female pushes the eggs out of her body, the male discharges his sperm right on top of them. Unlike the more uncertain spawning of fish and other sea animals, the frogs' way of mating always places the sperm and eggs close together. This improves the chances that the eggs will be fertilized.

In others, the male leaves a packet of sperm for the female to pick up.

Male centipedes wrap up their sperm in packets called *spermatophores.* The male spins a silken web and places his spermatophore on it. With the help of two fingerlike *gonopods,* the female pulls the spermatophore into an opening in her body where the eggs are fertilized. Many kinds of squids, octopuses, insects, and spiders also "hand off" their sperm in spermatophore packets.

And in many other animals, the male deposits his sperm directly inside the female's body.

In many species, the male is equipped with an organ called a *penis* and the female has a tube or cavity called a *vagina*. To transfer the sperm to the female, the male inserts his penis into the female's vagina. Special muscles force the sperm from the male's testes, through the penis, and into the vagina. Once the sperm enter the female's body, they swim to the eggs and fertilize them. This kind of mating is called *sexual intercourse* or *sex* and is used by most mammals, birds, and reptiles—and by many other kinds of animals, too.

Once a sperm and an egg join together, a new *embryo* begins to grow.

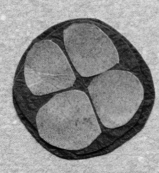
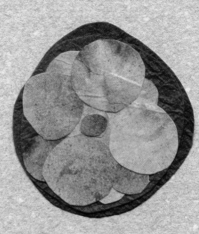
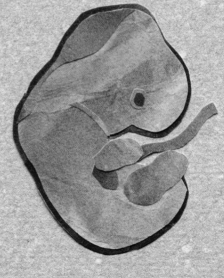

Unfertilized egg
Actual size: ⬝

Embryo at 2 days
Actual size: ◼

Embryo at 4 days:
Actual size: ◼

Embryo at 6 weeks
Actual size: 1/2 inch long

After fertilization, the egg cell divides into two cells and is now called an *embryo*. The cells of the embryo keep dividing and changing, staying together as they do. Bit by bit, the embryo grows and looks more and more like a baby animal. In some animals, such as shrews and mice, the embryo may take only twenty days or so to grow. In Asian elephants, the embryo grows for almost two years!

Embryo at 14 weeks
Actual size: 2" long

Chimpanzee born after 9 months

Some embryos grow all on their own.

After a female sea turtle mates, shells form around her fertilized eggs while they are still inside her body. The mom lays these eggs in a nest she digs on a sandy beach. Afterward, she crawls back into the ocean, swims away, and does nothing more for her young ones. The embryos grow independently, getting food and nourishment from the yolk sacs that are attached to them inside the eggshells.

Others receive constant nourishment from mom.

In tigers, humans, and most other mammals, embryos grow inside the mother's body in an organ called a *womb*. In the womb, the embryos receive a steady supply of nutrients from mom. These supplies reach the embryos through special tubes called *umbilical cords*. After an animal is born, its umbilical cord drops off, leaving a belly button at the point where the cord was attached.

When the embryos grow to a certain size or reach a certain age, they hatch . . .

Hatching, or getting out of an egg, can be a real challenge. To help it get out, a baby crocodile comes equipped with a special "egg tooth." This allows it to chip through the egg's tough shell. However, the eggs of many animals are not wrapped in hard shells. Fish, frogs, and other animals that grow in soft egg enclosures have a much easier time wriggling to freedom.

Or are born.

For embryos that develop inside the mother's body, the mother must give birth to release the young animals into the outside world. To force the babies out, the muscles around the mother's womb begin contracting, or tightening. This process is called *labor* and it helps slide the babies out of the womb. In cats, labor often lasts from six to eight hours. In other animals, labor can be shorter or longer.

Some look like their parents.

Others look a lot different.

Baby whales look like small versions of adult whales, but this isn't true of all animals. Many animals go through several life stages before they look like their parents. When butterfly eggs hatch, the babies that emerge are caterpillars. They must go through a change, or *metamorphosis*, before they become adult butterflies with wings.

But whatever they look like, they are now . . .

Babies! Ready to live, grow, and, one day . . .

Make their own babies.

Glossary

Asexual reproduction: reproduction in which a single parent makes new individuals or "babies" without combining eggs and sperm.

Budding: a form of asexual reproduction in which a special group of cells from an animal separates to become a new animal.

Cells: the tiny "building blocks" of which most living things are made.

Chromatophores: pigment cells in the skins of some animals that allow the animals to change their appearance.

Clone: a new individual made by asexual reproduction that is identical to its parent.

Eggs: special cells made in female ovaries, which are used in sexual reproduction.

Embryo: an animal in its earliest stage of development. Usually it begins growing from a fertilized egg.

Fertilization: the process of a sperm and an egg joining together.

Fission: a kind of asexual reproduction in which an animal divides to form two or more separate individuals.

Fragmentation: a kind of asexual reproduction in which pieces of an animal break off and grow into new individual animals.

Gonopods: tiny fingerlike appendages in some female animals that transfer the male's sperm packet into the female's body.

Labor: the process in which special muscles begin contracting to force a baby out of its mother's womb.

Mating: any of several ways by which a male animal passes its sperm to a female to fertilize her eggs.

Metamorphosis: a process in which animals change from one form into a form that is very different.

Ovary: an organ in females that produces eggs.

Penis: an organ that allows a male animal to place his sperm directly inside a female's body.

Sexual intercourse or sex: the process by which a male deposits sperm directly into a female's body, usually by inserting his penis into her vagina.

Sexual reproduction: reproduction in which sperm fertilize eggs and new babies begin to grow.

Spawn: to release sperm and eggs into the water.

Species: a group of related animals that share the same characteristics and are able to reproduce with one another.

Sperm: the special cells made in a male's testes that are used in sexual reproduction.

Spermatophore: a packet containing sperm that is produced by a male and transferred in some way to the female.

Testes: the male organs that produce sperm.

Umbilical cord: a special tube that transports blood and nutrients from a mother to an embryo inside the womb of mammals.

Vagina: the tube of a female where a male deposits his sperm during sexual intercourse.

Womb: the special organ in mammals, also called the uterus, where embryos develop until their birth.